YOUR KNOWLEDGE HAS VALUE

Otto Guggemos

St. Anselm and his fools in today's world

GRIN Verlag

Bibliografische Information der Deutschen Nationalbibliothek:

Die Deutsche Bibliothek verzeichnet diese Publikation in der Deutschen National-
bibliografie; detaillierte bibliografische Daten sind im Internet über http://dnb.d-
nb.de/ abrufbar.

Imprint:

Copyright © 1998 GRIN Verlag GmbH
Druck und Bindung: Books on Demand GmbH, Norderstedt Germany
ISBN: 978-3-640-88212-0

This book at GRIN:

http://www.grin.com/en/e-book/108849/st-anselm-and-his-fools-in-today-s-world

GRIN - Your knowledge has value

Der GRIN Verlag publiziert seit 1998 wissenschaftliche Arbeiten von Studenten, Hochschullehrern und anderen Akademikern als eBook und gedrucktes Buch. Die Verlagswebsite www.grin.com ist die ideale Plattform zur Veröffentlichung von Hausarbeiten, Abschlussarbeiten, wissenschaftlichen Aufsätzen, Dissertationen und Fachbüchern.

Visit us on the internet:

http://www.grin.com/

http://www.facebook.com/grincom

http://www.twitter.com/grin_com

ST. ANSELM AND HIS FOOLS IN TODAY'S WORLD

by

Otto Guggemos

INDS 681: The Gospel in the World of Thought

Christian Perspectives on the History of Philosophy

REGENT COLLEGE

April 1998

2

Convincitur ergo etiam insipiens esse vel in intellectu aliquid, quo nihil majus cogitari potest; quia hoc cum audit, intelligit; et quicquid intelligitur, in intellectu est. Et certe id, quo majus cogitari nequit, non potest esse in intellectu solo. Si enim vel in solo intellectu est, potest cogitari esse et in re: quod majus est. Si ergo id, quo majus cogitari non potest, est in solo intellectu, idipsum, quo majus cogitari non potest, est quo majus cogitari potest: sed certe hoc esse non potest. Existit ergo procul dubio aliquid, quo majus cogitari non valet, et in intellecu, et in re.[1]

INTRODUCTION

Not long ago, I met with some friends, Christians and non-Christians, for a philosophy discussion. We discussed Anselm of Canterbury's ontological argument for the existence of God. None of us was convinced that Anselm's proof was valid. In the beginning of the evening, we agreed with Schopenhauer who called Anselm's argument a "charming joke,_[2] but we went on talking and found ourselves challenged by Anselm's argument. It triggered a discussion that clarified various issues of our thoughts. This paper will be an investigation of the implications of Anselm's argument in the context of the contemporary western world -- an investigation of the multiple tangents from Anselm's philosophy to the streams of the popular mindsets of our time.

Anselm (1033/4-1109),[3] archbishop of Canterbury, lived in a time when many people felt that philosophical method possessed an intellectual respectability which theology lacked.[4] Some theologians called Dialectics, like Anselm, started to apply philosophical dialectic and logic to theological issues. The question of the time was how the independence of philosophy could be reconciled with the Catholic position. In 1072, Peter Damian defined philosophy as

---

[1]"Hence, even the fool is convinced that something exists in the understanding, at least, than which nothing greater can be conceived. For, when he hears of this, he understands it. And whatever is understood, exists in the understanding. And assuredly that, than which nothing greater can be conceived, cannot exist in the understanding alone. For, suppose it exists in the understanding alone: then it can be conceived to exist in reality; which is greater.

Therefore, if that, than which nothing greater can be conceived, exists in the understanding alone, the very being, than which nothing greater can be conceived, is one, than which a greater can be conceived. But obviously this is impossible. Hence, there is no doubt that there exists a being, than which nothing greater can be conceived, and it exists both in the understanding and in reality" (*Proslogium*, 2).

The translations I quote are those by Deane.

In all references to primary literature I will quote chapters, verses, numbers, etc. where possible. In secondary literature without paragraph numbering, I will cite by page numbers.

[2]Taylor, vii.
[3]Hauschild, 555.
[4]Evans, 11.

ancilla dominae (maid of the Lord).[5] Among the Dialectics, Anselm belonged to the group of the Realists.

About 1070 he started his writing career. His most important works are *Proslogium, Monologium,* and *Cur Deus homo.* Although calling Anselm the "father of Scholasticism_[6] might be an exaggeration, he set the trend in theology and philosophy for the following centuries by explaining the Christian faith in a rational, logical system.[7] In the 12th century, the Roman Catholic Church made him a saint, and in the 18th called him *doctor ecclesiae.*[8] Anselm became best known for the ontological argument for the existence of God which he first formulated in the *Proslogium.*[9] It goes as follows: God, Anselm defines, is the "being than which nothing greater can be conceived._[10] Since existence in reality is greater than existence in understanding alone, *i.,q.n.m.c.p.*[11] existing in reality is greater than *i.,q.n.m.c.p.* not existing in reality. Hence, if *i.,q.n.m.c.p.* existed not in reality, it were not *i.,q.n.m.c.p.,* for something greater than it could be conceived. This is an absurd contradiction in itself: "certe hoc esse non potest."[12] Quoting Psalm 14:1, Anselm says that even the fool who says in his heart, "There is no God,_ can conceive of *i.,q.n.m.c.p.,* for otherwise, he could not even make this statement about it/ him. Saying 'There is no God,' therefore is absurd, i.e. his non-existence is impossible, and hence his existence necessary.[13]

Our time has found many ways to say 'There is no God.' Psalm 14:1, and St. Anselm would call these people 'fools.' It sounds arrogant, but there is some of truth to it. In fact, 'foolishness' may be a clarifying concept to understand many features of the contemporary mindsets. Let us investigate whether and how Anselm's philosophy applies to modern and post-modern 'foolishness,' and what Anselm can contribute to twentieth century Christian thought.

A POST-MODERN PROOF

It is one of the dogmas of our time that one cannot prove the existence of God. It seems that before the Enlightenment, people believed in proofs for God's existence, and then Kant came and showed that they are all impossible.[14] However, the underlying issue is that it takes more

---

[5] Cambridge History, 792.
[6] Weisheipl, 304.
[7] He should rather be pre-Scholastic since he did not yet use the typical Scholastic method (Hauschild, 555).
[8] Weisheipl, 305.
[9] Cf. *Proslogium,* 2-4.
[10] *Proslogium,* 2: "id, quo nihil majus cogitari possit."
[11] In the following, I will simply use the abbreviation "*i.,q.n.m.c.p.*" for "*id, quo nihil majus cogitari possit.*"
[12] *Proslogium,* 2.
[13] Cf. Taylor, xvi.
[14] Kant, 2.2.2.3.3.-7.

4

than a proof to come to faith.[15] It takes conviction and repentance which are works of the
Holy Spirit. Paul expresses this when he points out that the "message of the cross is
foolishness to those who are perishing, but to us who are being saved it is the power of
God."[16] Paul sees Christians and non-Christians operating within different frames of
reference, and what is powerful in the one frame, is foolishness in the other.

Amselm makes a similar statement: The fool in Psalm 14:1 does not believe in God's
existence, precisely and only because he is a fool.[17] Anselm himself probably did not see that
it is a question of different frames of reference. He wants to make a philosophical proof,[18]
and calls anyone whom he could not convince not only foolish, but also "dull."[19] However,
by quoting Scripture the way he does, he makes his argument compatible to what
contemporary thought calls the hermeneutic circle. The Hebrew word for 'fool' in Psalm 14,
nabal, can also be translated 'ungodly person,'[20] i.e. somebody whose hermeneutic circle
excludes God. At the latest since Heidegger,[21] scholars are aware that all understanding is
interpretation influenced by the frames of reference we bring to it. A frame of reference
consists of previous understanding and interpretation. We interpret A according to how we
interpret B, B according to C, and C according to A, thus completing the circle. This
hermeneutic circle is the frame of reference in which discussion and understanding becomes
possible, but entering into a particular circle is a matter of faith. Science requires premises
which cannot be proved, and without which nothing can be proved.[22] Modern science and
scholarship works in the way that Anselm expressed: "Neque enim quaero intelligere, ut
credam; sed credo, ut intelligam. Nam et hoc credo, quia nisi credidero, non intelligam." --
"Unless I believed, I should not understand."[23]

Anselm's argument starts within subjectivity with the notion or concept of 'God' that we bear
within our minds. Therefore, it suits post-modern minds better than the arguments for the
existence of God that Christians traditionally use. The latter go along the line of the
cosmological and the teleological argument, which are proofs in Aquinas' *Summa Thelogica*[24]
and Anselm's *Monologium*. These arguments start with empirical data and argue that one can

---

[15]Cf. Lk 16: 31: "If they do not listen to Moses and the Prophets, they will not be convinced
even if someone rises from the dead."
[16]1Co 1:18.
[17]*Proslogium*, 3.
[18]Taylor, ix.
[19]*Proslogium*, 3. Deane's translation of *stultus*.
[20]Fohrer, 168.
[21]Cf. *Sein und Zeit*, 32 (p. 148 ff).
[22]Polanyi, 59f.
[23]*Proslogium*, 1. The entire quotation is in English: "For I do not seek to understand that I
may believe, but I believe in order to understand. For this I also believe, -- that unless I believed, I
should not understand."
[24]*Summa Theologica*, I,2.

only interpret them coherently if one postulates a god. Their basis are the data. Twentieth century scholarship in science and the arts has realized how the point of view always affects the shape even of these data,[25] and therefore criticizes the modernist trust in them. Anselm's proof does not rely on data, but begins with a faith commitment.

Any criticism of faith that claims faith is opposed to science, and that 'modern enlightened people' cannot believe in something that cannot be grasped by empirical and 'objective' research is not aware of this basic truth about science. Honest scientists know well that they are working inside a hermeneutic circle which is limited to the immanent world. It is foolish indeed to use science to refute metaphysical beliefs.

Another tangent exists between Anselm and the literary theories of structuralism (Claude Lévi-Strauss) and semiotics (Ferdinand de Saussure); they all make statements about reality by examining language.[26] As stated above, Anselm belonged to the philosophic Realists that followed Plato, Plotinus, and Augustine. Realists thought that the *universalia* (common nouns) were not abstractions of the individually existing things, but that the individual things participated in the reality of the general nouns. Thus, they argued that the common noun for a thing was 'more real' than the individual thing itself. These common nouns had first existed in God's mind, and are mirrored in the human mind and in God's creation.[27] Of course, modern linguists work without the premise of creation and outside the Neoplatonic framework. They seek knowledge of world-immanent structures by investigating the structures of language that pictures them. Anselm starts with *universalia* and goes beyond immanence into metaphysics, but like Saussure, Lévi-Strauss and others, he seeks knowledge by examining features of language.

DEFINITIONS OF 'GOD' AND REALITY

Today, the notion of 'reality' has become increasingly unclear. A fictional movie may be conceived as much more 'real' than an actual news clip. Various ideologies which are but fictional concepts have more influence on the world than any real person. The permanent confrontation with artificial food, materials, flowers, etc., and the imitation of 'real life' in the entertainment industry has created a hunger for 'the real thing,' but nobody can really say what 'real' really is. Anselm offers a definition of 'reality' we should consider.

Scholastic theory distinguishes between two types of existence: existence *in intellectu*, and existence *in re*. Something exists *in intellectu* when it "can be described and accurately

---

[25] Cf. Gadamer, 307-323.
[26] Cf. Griffith, 140-2.
[27] From c. 1090 on, the Realists were opposed by Nominalists who said that the common nouns were abstractions ("names_) of the true reality of every individual thing. For them, empirical

defined and the definitions and descriptions of them understood."[28] *In re* can be translated 'in reality.' In the Middle Ages, electromagnetic waves (presumably) existed *in re*, but not yet in the understanding, i.e. they were there, but nobody had concepts and notions that made it possible to think or talk about them. A square circle, in contrast, can be defined precisely, but its very definition excludes existence *in re*. The *universalia* are valid in both realms, which makes the two realms correspond and enables the *intellectum* to understand the *res*.

If we take away the idea of *universalia*, we see that this distinction is also valid outside a Neoplatonic framework. Nominalists[29] and Empiricists,[30] for instance, would regard existence *in intellectu* as the concepts we make to interpret the data our senses receive. The data would be perceptions of things that exist *in re*. The latter application might suit our purposes even better because it emphasizes the gulf between reality (*res*) and understanding (*intellectum*). The distinction defines reality as existence outside the intellect. If we understand something that really exists, then it exists in both realms. Saying that something 'really' exists therefore entails that it has an existence that is independent of our knowledge of it. Reality is the realm of being that exists independently of whether or not people know it. If the realm of reality is not entirely empty -- what Anselm certainly would deny --, his definition contradicts post-modern ideas like Michel Foucault's because it implies that 'truth' is more than a social construction which we make up for political or similar purposes. If something exists independently of our minds, then there is a truth about it, even if our interpretations of this truth may be ever so mistaken. This definition of 'reality' is useful, because it can conceive the reality of material beings, as well as of non-corporeal, and spiritual beings.

Many post-modern people who do not know of a reality outside of their minds feel the loneliness this produces. If there is nothing beyond oneself, and the concepts and imaginations of one's self, then one is alone in one's private universe. This is at the least one of the reasons for the renewed spiritual hunger of the "New Age."[31] More and more people have a desire for 'the real thing:' authentic experience of nature and spiritual things.[32] The progressing alienation in all features of modern life has given the word 'real' unpreceded fascination. Similarly, according to Anselm, it is better to exist in reality than only in the understanding (at least if the subject is good).

God is often understood as a mere projection -- a construct that is good and helpful to believe

---

facts outweighed rational arguments. About Realism cf. Hauschild, 553-5.
[28] Taylor, xiii.
[29] Cf. Hauschild 554.
[30] Cf. Solomon/ Higgins, 194ff.
[31] Cf. Solomon/ Higgins, 304. What Solomon and Higgins call "hunger for philosophy" should better be termed "hunger for spirituality."

in. This does not mean that God does not exist at all, but that he only exists in the understanding. Popular pluralist theory holds that it is irrelevant whether or not God exists in reality, as long as he exists in understanding. Many would say that God is a helpful imaginative tool for religious people, even if they are religious, themselves. Existence in reality would compete with other religious convictions, whereas limiting God's existence to the imagination allows every person to create his or her own reality.

Let us now try to define the notion of 'God.'[33] The attributes of God that can be found in different religious traditions are: infinity, unity, simplicity, incorporeality, immutability, impassability, eternity, goodness, omniscience, and omnipotence.[34] It is reasonable to assume that a being which unites all these attributes in itself would be the greatest being, one could think of, *i.,q.n.m.c.p.* Unity, simplicity, immutability, and impassability make this being reliable. The Greek God's lacked unity, they fought each other, and human beings could never be sure of which party they could rely on. Lack of impassability, i.e. that something can cause God to change, would entail that God were not ultimately free, and could be manipulated like pagan idols.

The biggest philosophical problem is to conceive of an omnipotent, omniscient, and all-good being. The existence of evil seemingly makes one of them impossible. Either evil exists because God cannot overcome it, or evil exists because God does not know it, or he permits evil because he is not all good.[35] The Bible solves this dilemma by introducing the attribute of love, God's love even for the evildoer, and the concept of a salvation history. God can and will overcome evil, but he grants time for evildoers to repent, because he loves them.[36] Another attribute of God is creator and sustainer. For Anselm as a Neoplatonist, every other being is defined by *i.,q.n.m.c.p.*, "for in him we live and move and have our being."[37] God is the supreme being from whom all other existence comes. This is linked to infinity, i.e. there is no place and no existence that is not affected by *i.,q.n.m.c.p.*

These attributes become irrelevant if God has no existence that is independent of human understanding of him. Most obviously, he could be manipulated as the believer pleases, and he could not give the stability for which believers long. God's knowledge and God's power would be limited to the knowledge and the power of the believer, who is hardly omnipotent or omniscient. Moreover, something that exists only within the believer cannot have a

---

[32] Cf. the renewed boom of natural products
[33] Cf. for this and the following paragraph *Proslogium*, 6-20.
[34] Owen, 346f.
[35] Owen, 347.
[36] This is not a concluding answer to the problem of theodicy, but a sketchy summary of the answers given in the Christian tradition. Cf. Owen (347): "Christians believe that God displays his omnipotence by *overcoming* evil through the ministry of Christ."
[37] Ac 17:28.

goodness that is substantially better than that of the believer. Of course, a God limited to a mere concept *in intellectu* cannot be eternal. They presuppose people who have the concept and can neither have existed before mankind, not after it. God's existence would cease when people believe in him.[38] The problem at stake is that we cannot believe in a creator, and believe that we have created him ourselves at the same time. In addition, we cannot believe in somebody who carries us, when we believe that it is ultimately us who carry him.

Finally, a living and loving relationship presupposes that there is somebody who is capable of interaction. We cannot interact properly with somebody who merely exists in our understanding. For an I-Thou-relationship, we need a real person.

If God exists only in understanding, he is an idol. Idolatry certainly is foolish, because it means worshipping something that is a mere projection that we produce ourselves. Here, the critique of Ludwig Feuerbach hits its target. Anselm's definition of God as *i.,q.n.m.c.p.* exposes relativist theology as idolatry, and shows its foolishness.

OTHER FOOLS

People who do not see themselves as religious tend to have a different concept of God. They would say that statements about God and his existence look like meaningful statements only at first sight, but at closer examination, it does not really matter, whether or not they are true. For example, Antony Flew compares God to a gardener. He tells the story a man who asserts that a beautiful place he finds on an island must be tended by a gardener because it is so ordered.[39] His companion explains the same phenomenon as naturally grown, and denies the hypothesis of a gardener. The former man tries to prove his assertion, but he cannot, because he never beholds or even finds any positive trace of the gardener. Flew makes the point that, at the end of the day, there is really no difference between a "invisible, intangible, eternally elusive gardener" and "no gardener at all."[40]

However, if we follow Anselm's definition of God as '*i.,q.n.m.c.p.*,' Flew is not talking about God at all. Undoubtedly, Flew can conceive of many beings that are greater than what he calls 'God.' Moreover, the men in the parable could easily imagine their own existence without this gardener. They could not talk about the gardener in this mode, if they were part of the garden. Then, the existence of the gardener would immediately matter to them.

It is interesting to compare Gaunilon's critique[41] of Anselm's argument. Gaunilon reduces

---

[38] Friedrich Nietzsche was the first to put his finger on this implication of modern philosophy. 'God is dead, and we have killed him' (The Gay Science, 181)

[39] Allen/ Springsted, 281-4, from: New Essays in Philosophical Theology. eds. Antony Flew and Alasdair MacIntyre, 1955 and 1983.

[40] Allen/ Springsted, 302.

[41] Gaunilon, a contemporary of Anselm wrote the *Liber pro Insipiente* (In Behalf of the Fool)

Anselm's argument *ad absurdum*, saying that although we can conceive of a utopic island which is greater than any island any human ever saw, it does not necessarily exist in reality.[42] If this were true, we could define anything into real existence by raising it to the superlative. For Anselm, however, there is at least one being that is greater than the greatest island that can be conceived: *i.,q.n.m.c.p.* Anselm's proof works only for the one greatest conceivable being, and not for the superlative of every single category. Because we can conceive of something greater than the most blessed island, its existence, just as the existence of aliens (to give a contemporary example) is indifferent to our existence, whereas the existence of God is not.

Furthermore, there are those contemporaries for whom the notion of God necessarily includes that he does n̲o̲t̲ exist in reality. Like any ideology, God exists *in intellectu*, and thus he is important, but (for various reasons) they are sure that he is not more than a projection. Anselm's work clarifies all these positions which think of God as not existing in reality. Like Flew's God, these Gods do not deserve the name 'God' according to Anselm's definition. The case of Gaunilon indicates that a being which someone conceives as not existing in reality is not *i.,q.n.m.c.p* for him. It is a tautology that *i.,q.n.m.c.p.* cannot but exist in reality, because where it does not, the person can conceive of something greater which then is *i.,q.n.m.c.p.* for the person. Everybody has a limit, whence he cannot think of something greater. Therefore, in Anselm's definition, we must call the being of which a person cannot conceive anything greater, as the God of this person. Whatever someone relies on, and whatever someone lives for, that is his or her God. Thus, it is simply nonsense when "the fool says in his heart 'There is no God.'" Where his heart is, there is his God,[43] he just happens to use another name for his God, but he certainly has something which he conceives as the greatest being -- the being which defines his life. This foolishness becomes obvious when we consider what kinds of beings are the greatest being people can conceive, which they put their trust, and invest their lives in. There are many people for whom their home country, the stock market, romantic love, their family, or their pets are what really give their lives meaning, direction and value. They might not call it 'God', but they believe it is *i.,q.n.m.c.p.*, and live as if there were nothing greater.

The problem is that there can only be one legitimate *i.,q.n.m.c.p.* If A can conceive of nothing greater than love, B can conceive of nothing greater than philosophy, and C can conceive of nothing greater than Jesus Christ, then at least two of them are wrong: If love, philosophy and Jesus Christ are equally great, then all three are mistaken. If the three ideas are subordinate to

---

as a response to Anselm's *Proslogion* (cf. Deane, 145).
[42]Cf. *Liber pro Insipiente*, 6.

each other, then the understanding of two of them is too limited to conceive of the being which really is greater than what they think of as *i.,q.n.m.c.p.* One can conceive of something greater than what the others think of as *i.,q.n.m.c.p.*, but they don not conceive of it because they are fools.

Post-modern relativism would deny this kind of logic. They accept contradicting truth claims as not mutually exclusive. The underlying theory is that there is no absolute truth, but only subjective 'truths.' However this sentence is already an absolute truth claim, and this kind of radical pluralism deconstructs itself. In fact, the philosophy of pluralism has its own values that its promoters hold important enough to impose on others. A quotation from a post-modern book about philosophy is very revealing: After attacking contemporary ivory-towered philosophy for having lost its connection to life, and indulging in dogmatic debates on details, the writers conclude "What we need is not more hardheadedness but more humaneness, more openness."[44] Obviously, they hold something like humaneness or tolerance as *i.,q.n.m.c.p.*, and they were fools to say 'There is no *i.,q.n.m.c.p.* independent of human understanding.'[45]

The problem is best seen in the field of ethics and morals. Pluralist societies are facing the difficulty that any moral code is based on a world view.[46] How one views the world is inseparable linked to what one understands as *i.,q.n.m.c.p.* Whatever *i.,q.n.m.c.p.* is, it functions as the ultimate goal and legitimization of a person's behavior. A vivid example is the dilemma of the western world which urges the People's Republic of China to be tolerant of its minorities, and the Chinese government replies that the western world should tolerate the fact that tolerance is not part of the Chinese Communist system.

Some post-modern philosophers go so far that they even deem communication of meaningful statements impossible. If *i.,q.n.m.c.p.* can be X for one person, and Y for another, then they have a barrier in their communication, because they fill the same notion with something different. When they talk about *i.,q.n.m.c.p.,* they cannot understand each other. Jaques Derrida states "Il n'y a pas de hors-texte [sic!]."[47] The problem is that if he is right, we can never be sure what he meant by that. It seems fair to call these strange blossoms foolishness, because they are the end of all meaningful conversation and real understanding.

"The fool says in his heart, 'There is no God;'" in other words: there is no being of which nothing greater can be conceived. Under Anselm's definition of God, this is inconsistent and

---

[43] Cf. Mt 6:21.
[44] Solomon/ Higgins, 305.
[45] If they grant that there may be something greater that what they deem as *i.,q.n.m.c.p.*, they assert that no one has yet conceived of it.
[46] Cf. MacIntyre, esp. p. 216.
[47] "There is nothing outside the text;" cited from Wilson, 58.

'foolish' in whatever way we interpret it.

CONCLUSION

After all, what does Anselm actually prove? -- He shows that one cannot believe in God without saying that God exists independently of himself. This is tautological, but profound. At the philosophy discussion mentioned above, we discovered something interesting: Those who believed in God could theoretically conceive of the case that God would not exist, but none of them could tell what it would take for him to be convinced of God's non-existence. Antony Flew poses the question: "What would have to occur or to have occurred to constitute for you a disproof of the love of, or of the existence of, God?" The answer is: Nothing. We have talked about the hermeneutic circle. There is nothing which can disprove the frame of reference because all data are collected and interpreted within the frame, and are perceived as fitting into it. The frame of reference is defined by *i.,q.n.m.c.p.*, and defines what *i.,q.n.m.c.p.* is, therefore, *i.,q.n.m.c.p.* is axiomatic and cannot be disproved.

Another question: What does it do to God when he does not exist outside the imagination? If it is a good religion, then believing in him is a helpful hypothesis. It is certainly better for the personal well-being, and the well-being of a society to believe in a transcendent loving God, who calls humans to neighborly love and accountability than to put one's trust in money, which calls its followers to greed and selfishness. But this practical calculation is not enough. The hypothesis works only if the believers do not take it as a hypothesis, but as true in reality. One cannot believe that his God sustains him, and believe that he himself sustains his God. Believing in God necessarily includes believing that his existence is independent from the believer. One cannot carry the God whom he needs to carry him. It is foolish to seek spirituality without claiming reality.

Herein lies one of the great tensions within post-modernity. On the one hand, there is a renewed hunger for spirituality after science lost the fascination it had in the modern era and dangers of great ideologies have become clear. More and more people ask questions about faith and the meaning of life.[48] On the other hand, people are reluctant to accept the possible answers, because they contain absolute truth claims. Any answer that could possibly answer these questions would contain a truth claim about the identity of *i.,q.n.m.c.p.*, and hence compete with other claims. It is foolish to want both -- relativism and faith.

So, what does it take to come to faith if a proof is not enough? -- A miracle. John 3 describes it as a new birth, because when the being that functions as *i.,q.n.m.c.p.* is re-identified, the whole paradigm within which a person lives and thinks shifts. Granted, evidence can

12

question an existing framework, but to leave it, a leap of faith is required. A proof is not enough. Søren Kierkegaard was the philosopher who spelled this out for the modern era: "The decision lies in the subject."[49] Believing in God implies his existence *in re*. In order to believe in him, we must believe in his existence *in re*, and in order to discern his existence *in re*, we have to believe in him. Only if we believe can we understand and behave sensibly, or know what we live for. Only the fool thinks that there is no supreme being, and the denial of the reality of a supreme being produces foolishness.

Gratias tibi, bone Domine, gratias tibi; quia quod prius credidi, te donante, jam sic intelligo, te illuminante; ut si te esse nolim credere, non possim non intelligere.[50]

---

[48]Cf. Solomon/ Higgins, 304.
[49]Allen/ Springsted, 223, from Concluding Unscientific Postscript, by Søren Kierkegaard. trans. David F. Swenson and Walter Lowrie, 1941 and 1069.
[50]"I thank thee, gracious Lord, I thank thee; because what I formerly believed by thy bounty, I now so understand by thine illumination, that if I were unwilling to believe that thou dost exist, I should not be able to understand this to be true" (*Proslogium*, 4).

BIBLIOGRAPHY

Allen, Diogenes and Eric O. Springsted (eds.) Primary Readings in Philosophy for Understanding Theology. Leominster, England: Gracewing and Louisville, Kentucky: Westminster/ John Knox, 1992.

Deane, S.N. (trans.) St. Anselm: Basic Writings: Proslogium, Monologium, Gaunilon's In Behalf of the Fool, and Cur Deus homo. La Salle, Ill.: Open Court, 1962.

Evans, G. R. Anselm and Talking about God. Oxford: Clavendon Press, 1978.

Fohrer, Georg. *Hebräisches und aramäisches Wörterbuch zum Alten Testament*. Berlin and New York: de Gruyter, ^{2}1989.

Gadamer, Hans-Georg. *Wahrheit und Methode: Grundzüge einer philosophischen Hermeneutik*. Tübingen: Mohr (Siebeck), 1972.

Griffith, Kelley, Jr. Writing Essays About Literature: A Guide and Style Sheet. San Diego, New York, Chicago, Austin, Washington, DC, London, Sydney, Tokyo, Toronto: Harcourt Brace Jovanovich, ^{3}1990.

Haas, Carolus (ed.) *Sancti Anselmi Cantuariensis Monologium et Proslogion nec non Liber pro Insipiente cum Libro Apologetico*. Tübingen: Laupp, 1868.

Hauschild, Wolf-Dieter. *Lehrbuch der Kirchen- und Dogmengeschichte*, vol. 1, *Alte Kirche und Mittelalter*. Gütersloher Verlagshaus, 1995.

Heidegger, Martin. *Sein und Zeit*. Tübingen: Niemeyer, 1953.

Kant, Immanuel. *Kritik der reinen Vernunft*, ed. Benno Erdmann. Hamburg and Leipzig: Voss, ^{3}1884.

Owen, H.P. "God, Concepts of," Encyclopedia of Philosophy, ed. Paul Edwards. New York: Macmillan and London: Collier Macmillan, 1967, II 344-6.

Nietzsche, Friedrich. The Gay Science, trans. W. Kaufmann. New York: Random House, 1974.

MacIntyre, Alasdair. After Virtue: A Study in Moral Theory. Notre Dame, Indiana: University Press, ^{2}1984.

Plantinga, Alvin. God and Other Minds: A Study of the Rational Justification of Belief in God. Ithaca, N.Y.: Cornell University, 1967.

Polanyi, Michael. Personal Knowledge: Towards a Post-Critical Philosophy. New York and Evanston: Harper & Row, 1964.

Solomon, Robert C. and Kathleen M. Higgins. A Short History of Philosophy. New York and Oxford: Oxford University Press, 1996.

Tanner, J.R., C.W. Previtte-Orton and Z.N. Brooke (eds.). The Cambridge Medieval History, vol. 5, Contest of Empire and Papacy. Cambridge: University Press, 1968.

Taylor, Richard. "Introduction,_ in The Ontological Argument: From St. Anselm to Contemporary Philosophers, ed. Alvin Plantinga. London and Melbourne: Macmillan, 1968, vii-xviii.

Weisheipl, James A. "Anselm,_ The Encyclopedia of Religion, vol. 1. New York: Macmillan and London: Collier Macmillan, 1987.

Wilson, Edward O. "Back from Chaos," The Atlantic Monthly, Mar 1998.